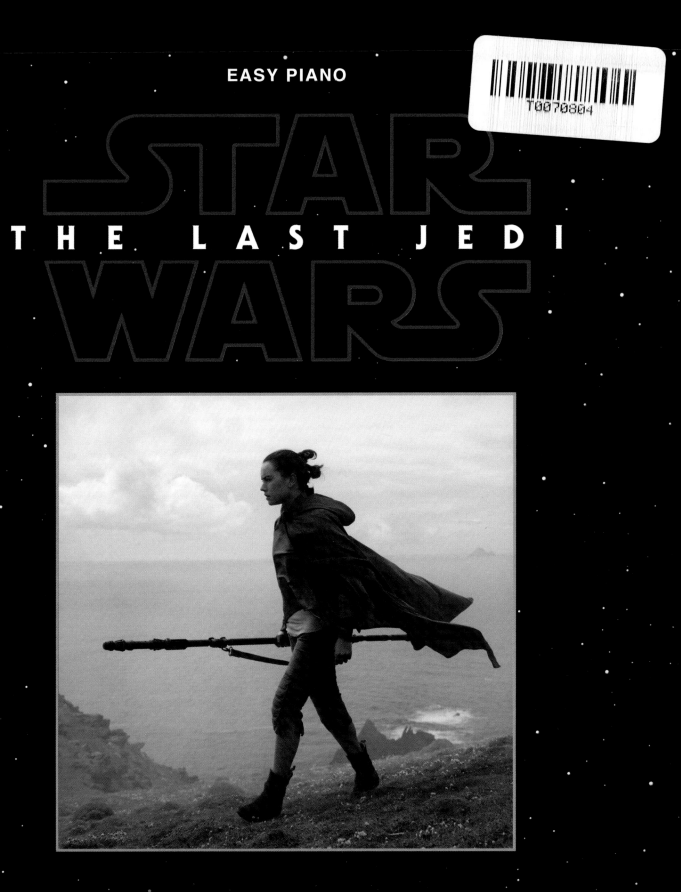

EASY PIANO

STAR WARS
THE LAST JEDI

ISBN 978-1-5400-2101-4

© 2018 & TM Lucasfilm Ltd. All Rights Reserved.

HAL•LEONARD®

7777 W. BLUEMOUND RD. P.O. BOX 13819 MILWAUKEE, WI 53213

In Australia Contact:
Hal Leonard Australia Pty. Ltd.
4 Lentara Court
Cheltenham, Victoria, 3192 Australia
Email: ausadmin@halleonard.com.au

For all works contained herein:
Unauthorized copying, arranging, adapting, recording, Internet posting, public performance,
or other distribution of the printed music in this publication is an infringement of copyright.
Infringers are liable under the law.

Visit Hal Leonard Online at
www.halleonard.com

MAIN TITLE *AND* ESCAPE

Music by JOHN WILLIAMS

Moderately

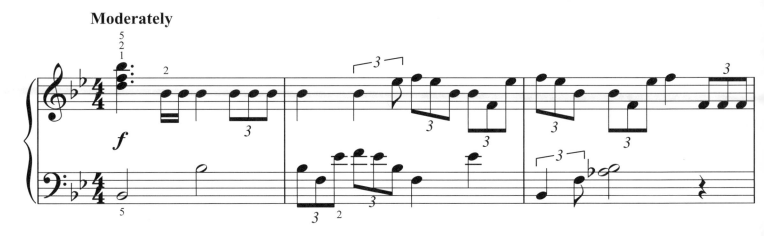

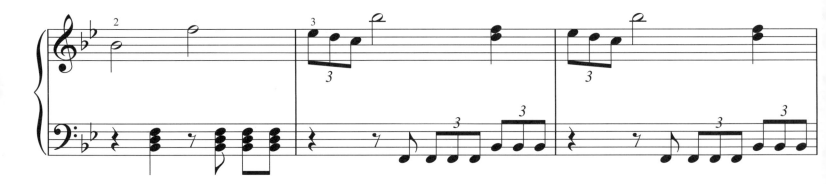

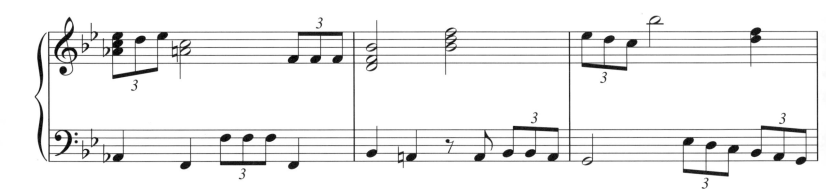

© 2017 Utapau Music, Bantha Music and Warner-Tamerlane Publishing Corp.
All Rights Reserved.   Used by Permission.

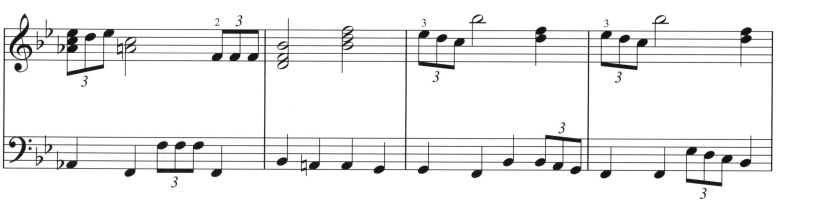

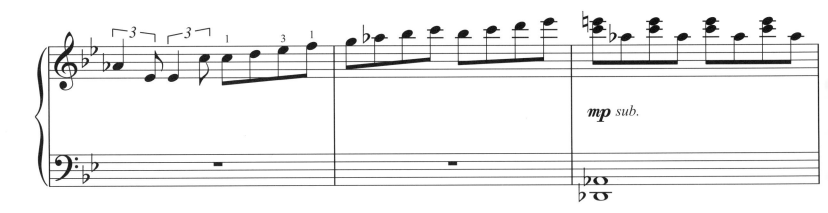

Moderately slow, expressively

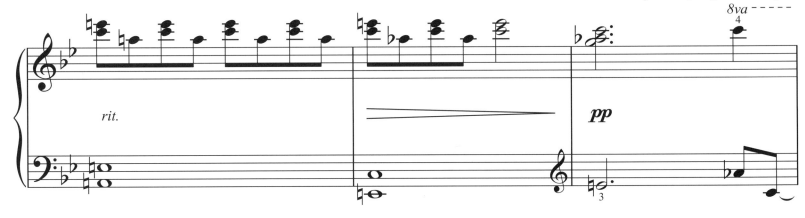

Moderately, steadily

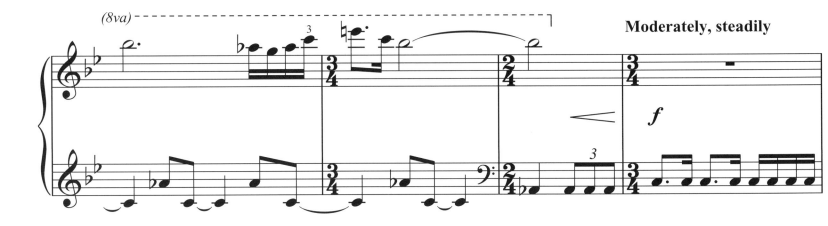

AHCH-TO ISLAND

Music by JOHN WILLIAMS

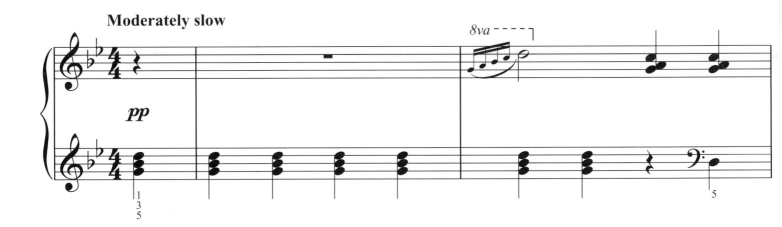

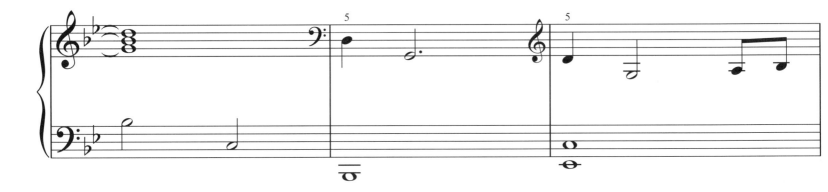

© 2017 Utapau Music, Bantha Music and Warner-Tamerlane Publishing Corp.
All Rights Reserved.   Used by Permission.

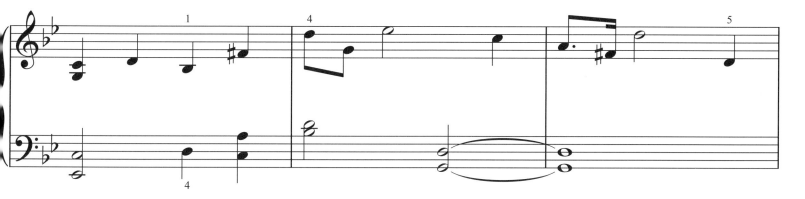

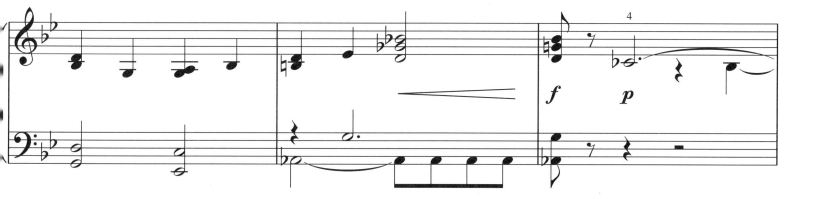

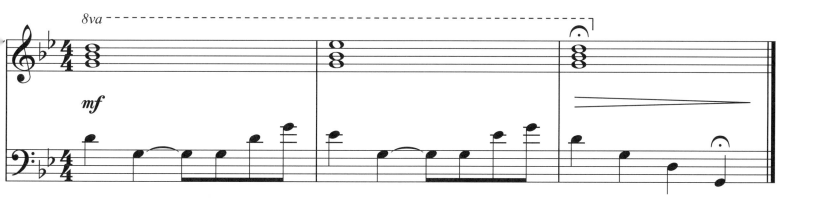

THE SUPREMACY

Music by JOHN WILLIAMS

Quickly

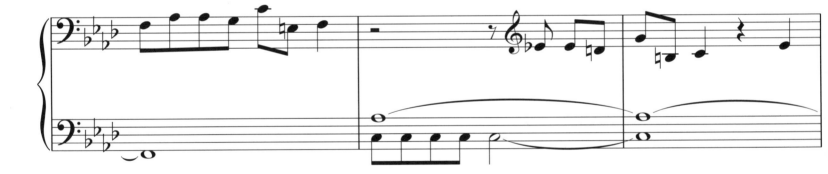

Moderately slow, expressively

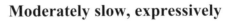

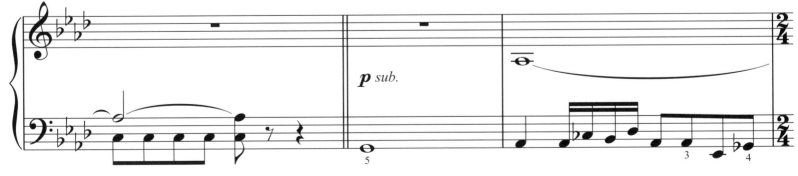

© 2017 Utapau Music, Bantha Music and Warner-Tamerlane Publishing Corp.
All Rights Reserved.   Used by Permission .

Faster

Moderately, steadily

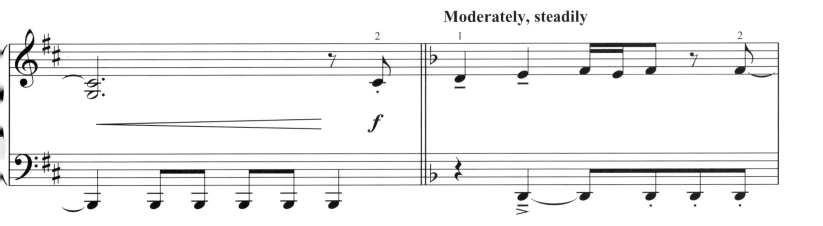

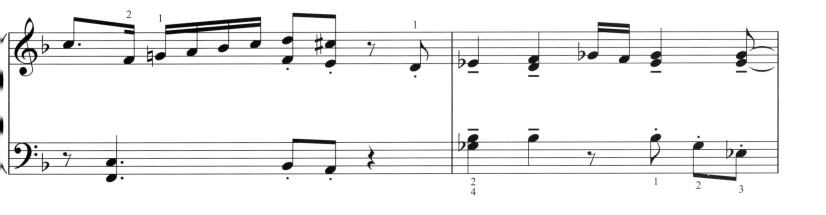

THE REBELLION IS REBORN

Music by JOHN WILLIAMS

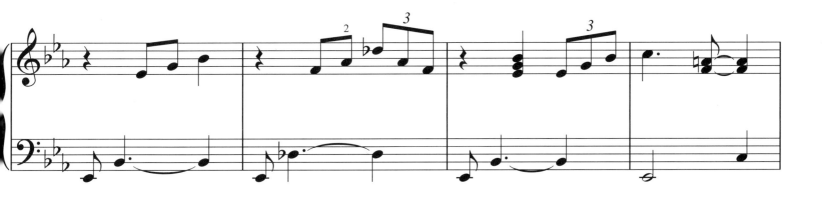

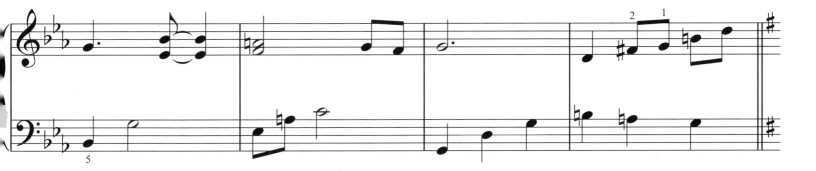

© 2017 Utapau Music
All Rights Reserved. Used by Permission.

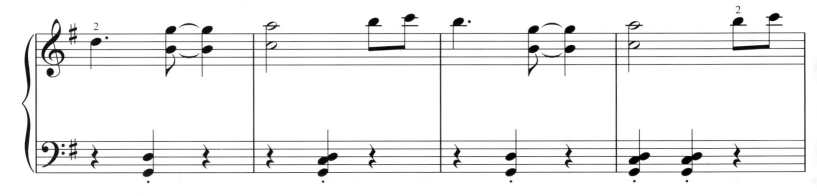

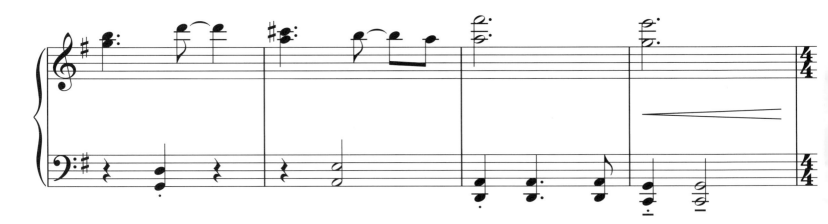

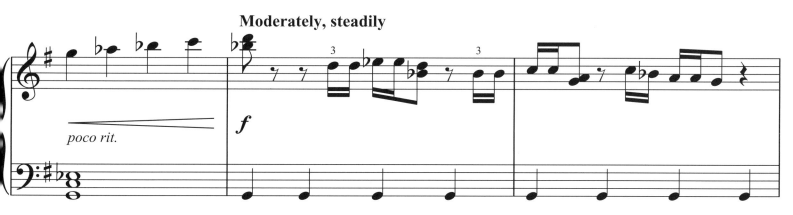

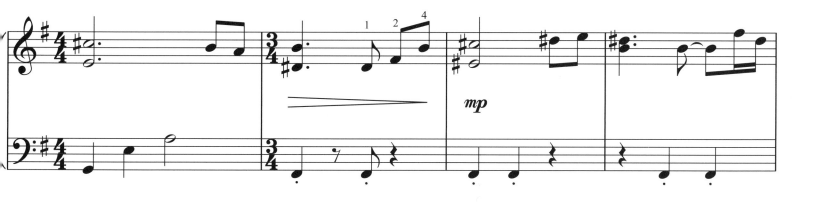

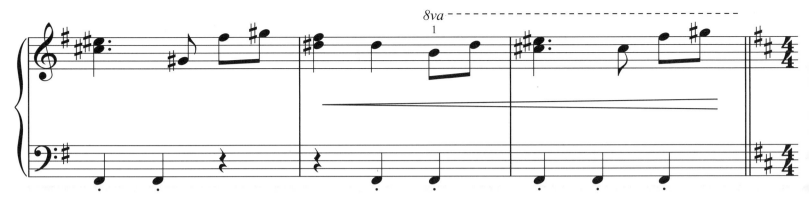

Moderately, steadily

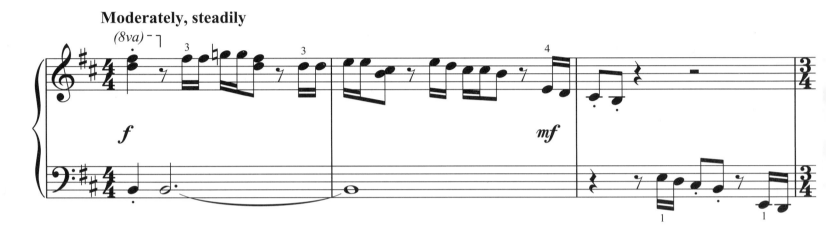

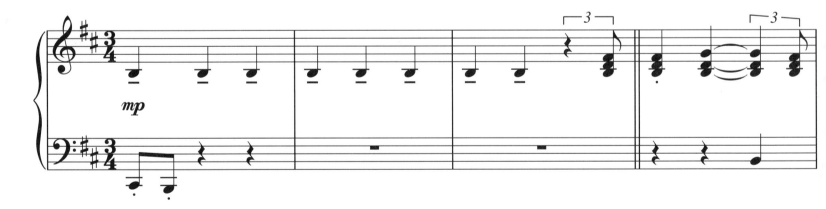

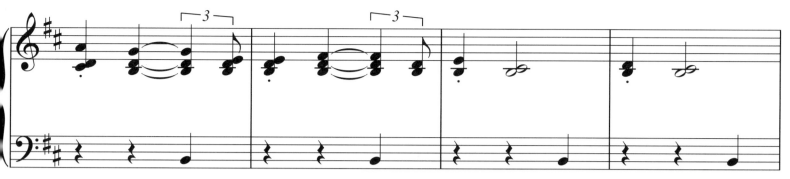

cresc.

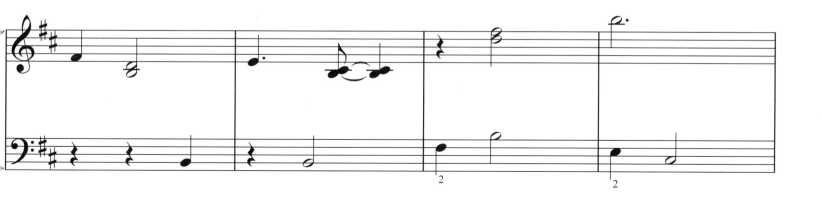

24

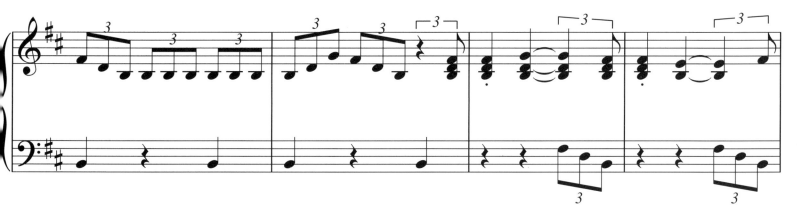

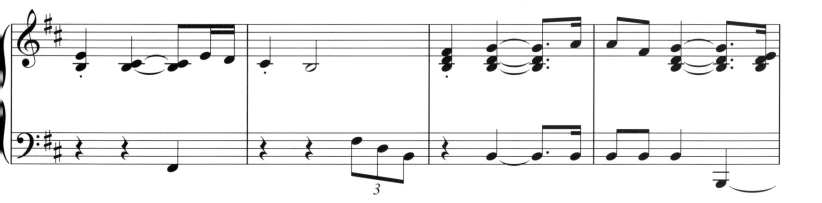

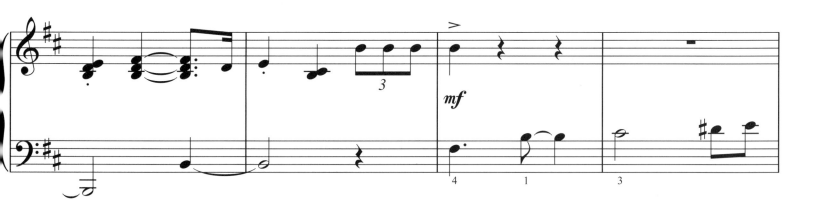

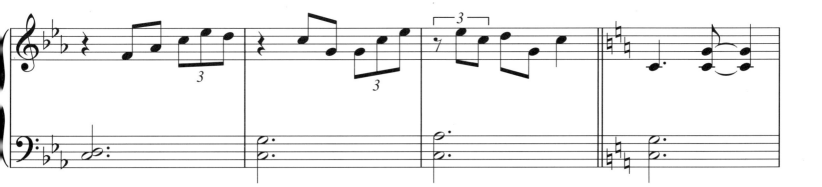

FUN WITH FINN AND ROSE

Music by JOHN WILLIAMS

Moderately slow, expressively

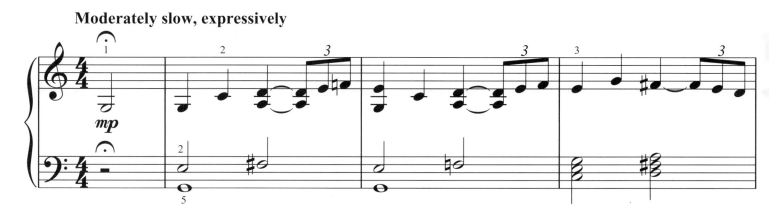

Slightly slower

Moderately

© 2017 Utapau Music, Bantha Music and Warner-Tamerlane Publishing Corp.
All Rights Reserved.   Used by Permission.

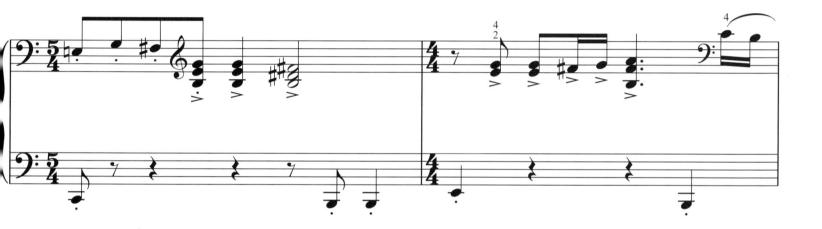

Moderately slow, expressively

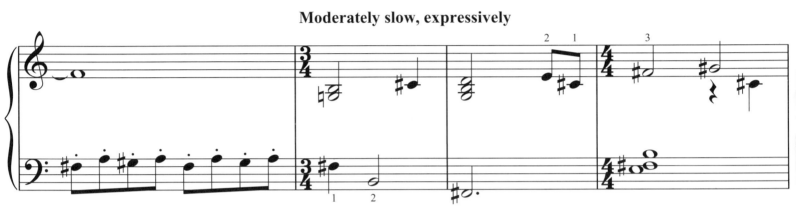

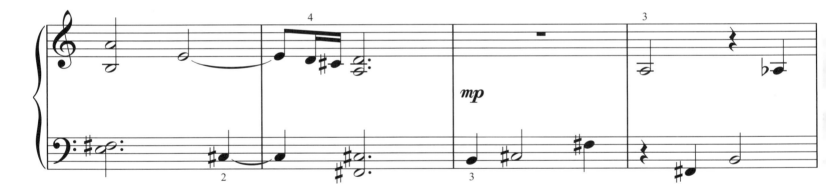

Moderately slow

Moderately, in 2

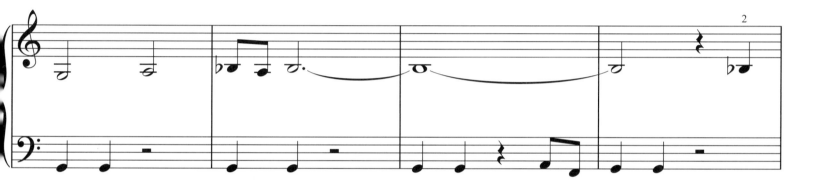

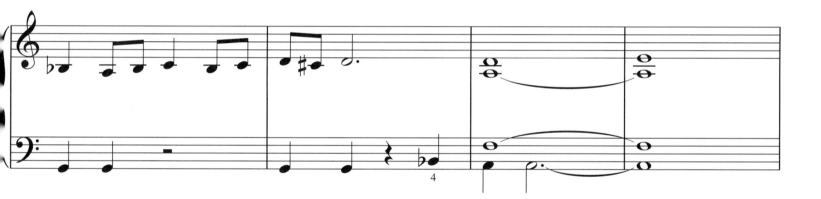

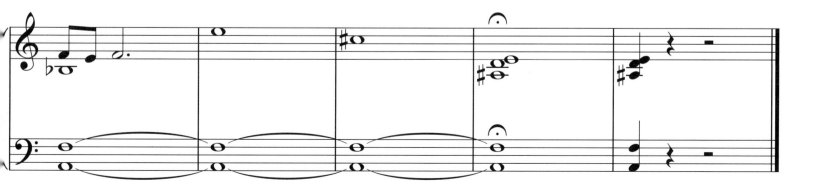

OLD FRIENDS

Music by JOHN WILLIAMS

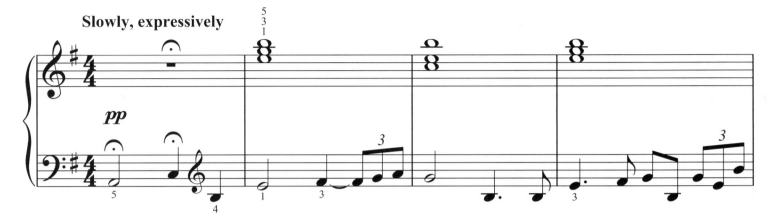

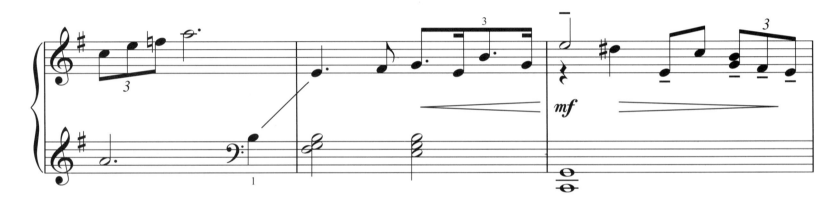

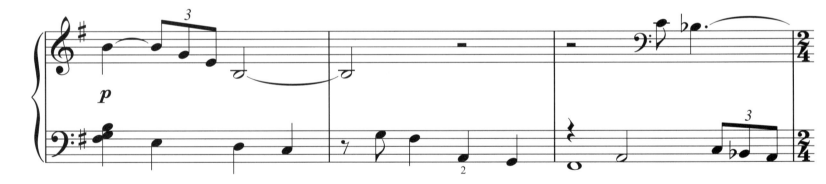

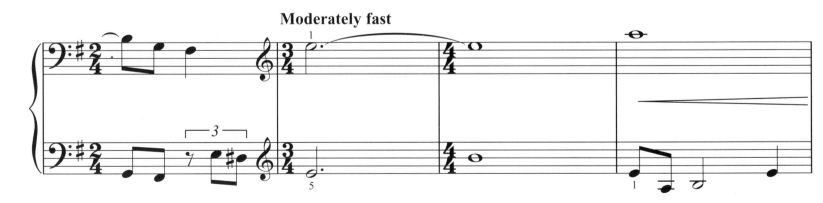

© 2017 Utapau Music, Bantha Music and Warner-Tamerlane Publishing Corp.
All Rights Reserved.   Used by Permission.

Largo

Moderately slow, expressively

CANTO BIGHT

Music by JOHN WILLIAMS
Includes excerpt from "Aquarela Do Brasil"
Written by ARY BARROSO

Quickly (♩ = 104)

© 2017 Utapau Music
Excerpt from "Aquarela Do Brasil" published by Peer International Corporation obo Irmãos Vitale SA Comércio & Indústria
All Rights Reserved.   Used by Permission.

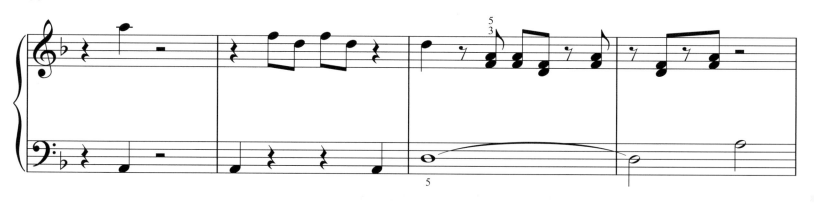

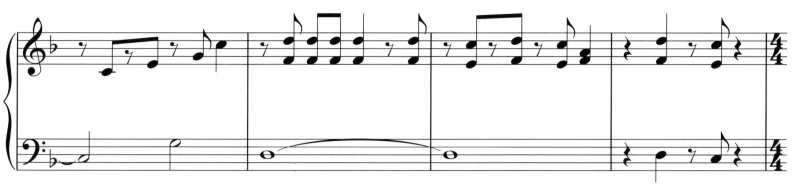

Moderately fast (♪♪ = ♪♪³)

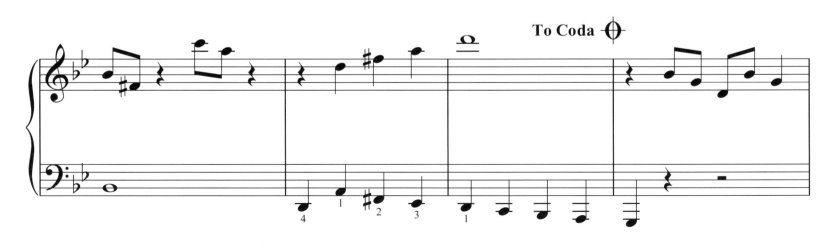

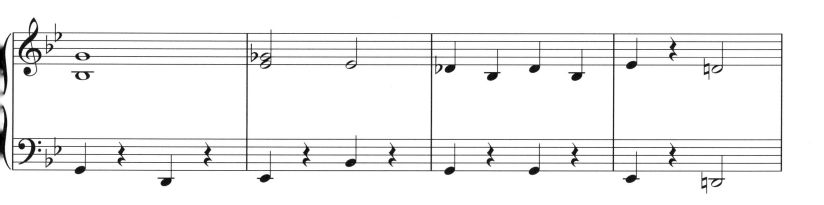

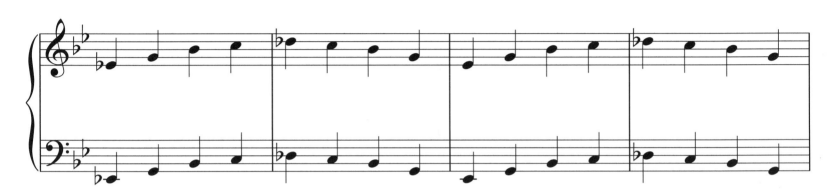

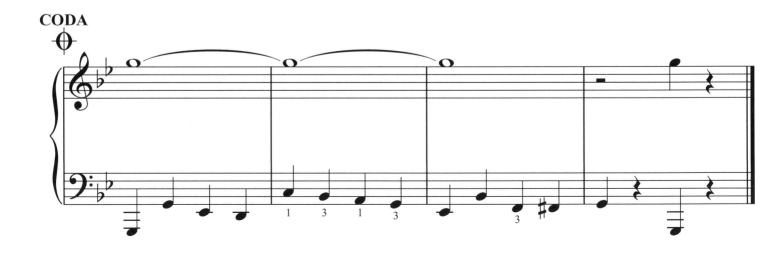

THE SACRED JEDI TEXTS

Music by JOHN WILLIAMS

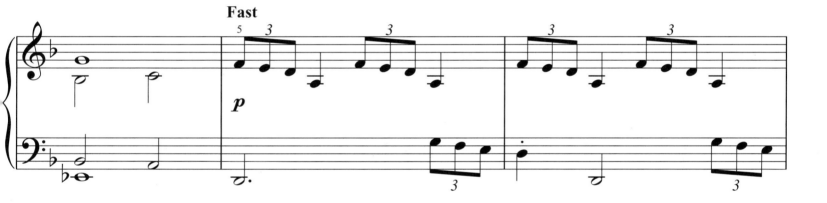

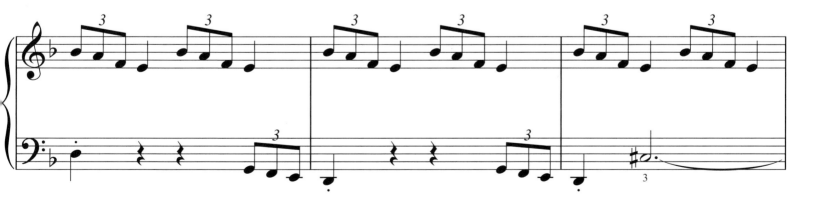

© 2017 Utapau Music, Bantha Music and Warner-Tamerlane Publishing Corp.
All Rights Reserved. Used by Permission.

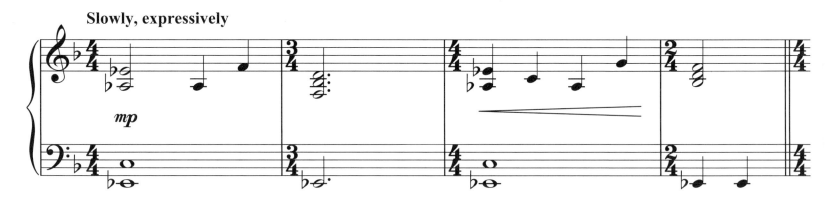

Slowly, expressively

Moderately

Slower

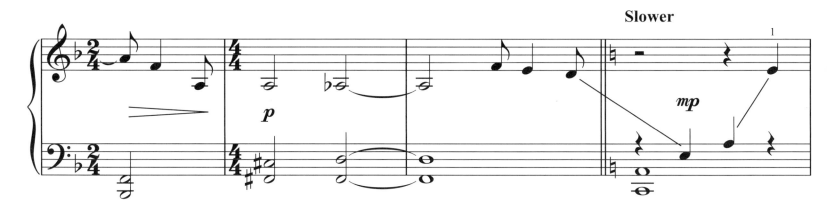

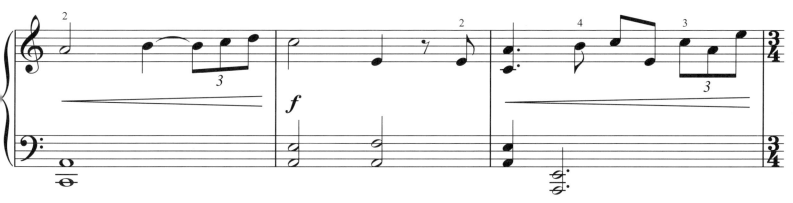

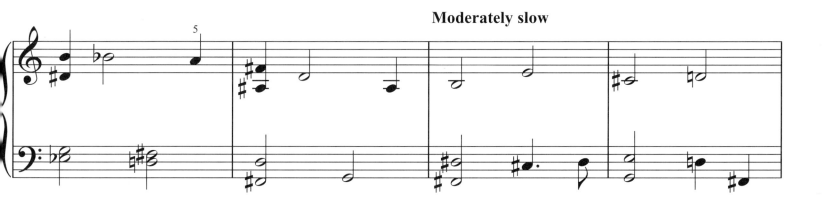

44

Slowly, freely

Moderately

Slowly

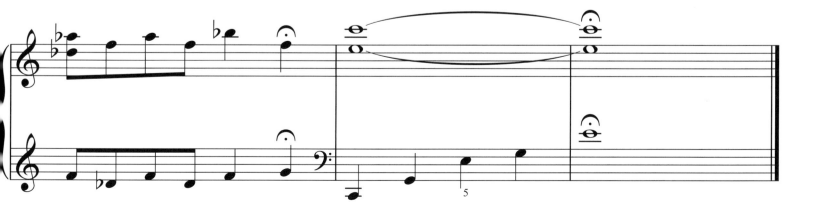

THE BATTLE OF CRAIT

Music by JOHN WILLIAMS

Slowly, expressively

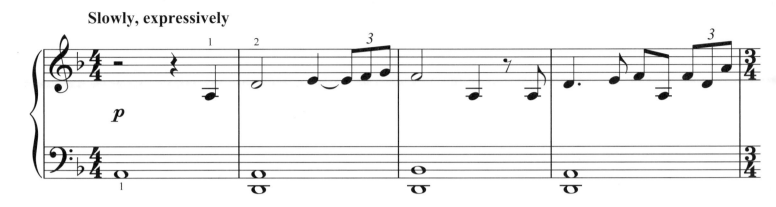

Moderately, deliberately

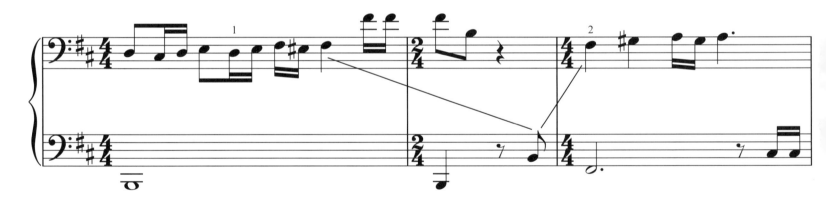

© 2017 Utapau Music, Bantha Music and Warner-Tamerlane Publishing Corp.
All Rights Reserved. Used by Permission.

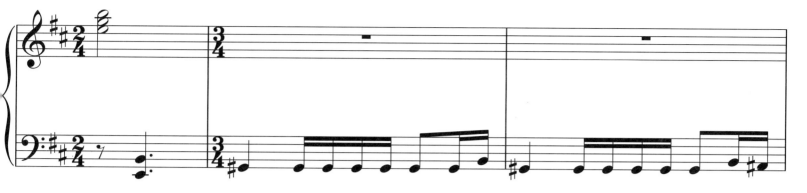

Faster

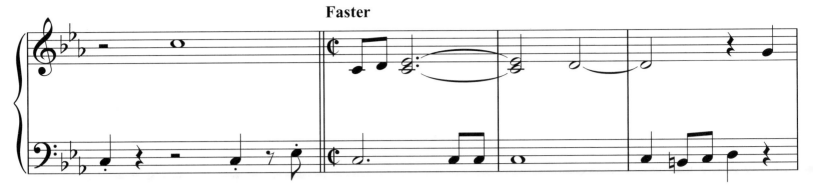

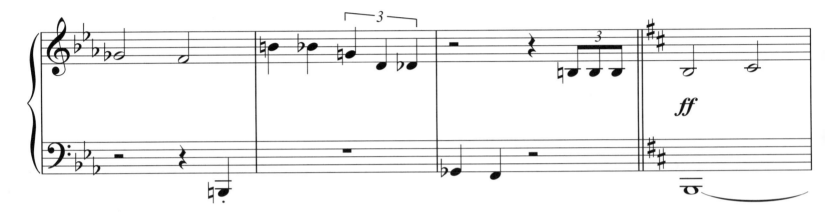

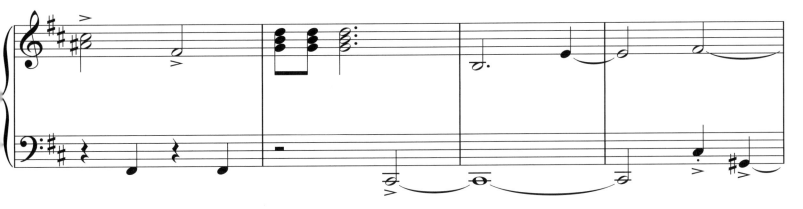

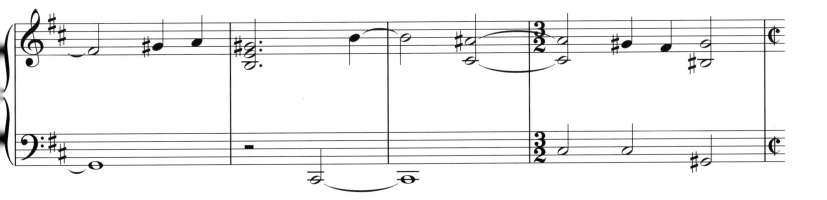

THE SPARK

Music by JOHN WILLIAMS

Moderately slow

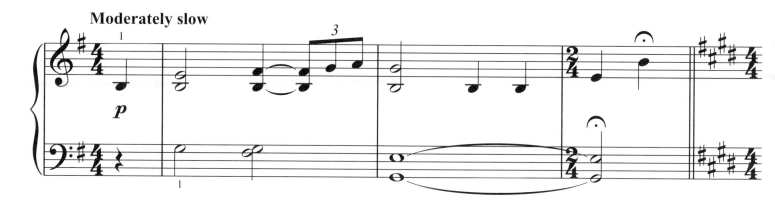

Slightly faster, expressively

poco rall.

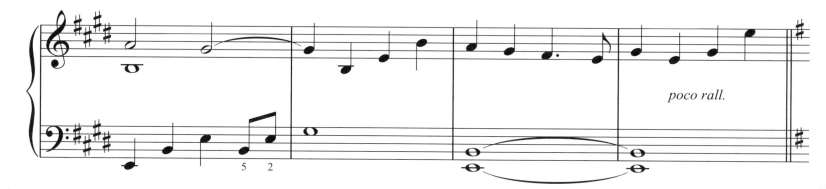

© 2017 Utapau Music, Bantha Music and Warner-Tamerlane Publishing Corp.
All Rights Reserved. Used by Permission.

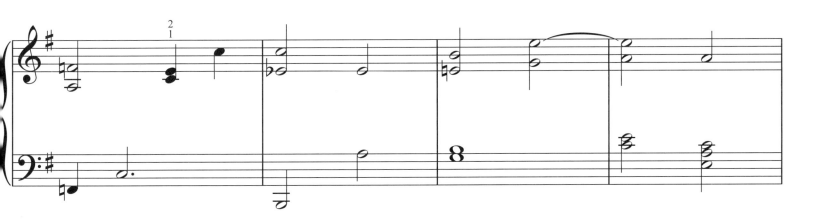

Slowly, expressively

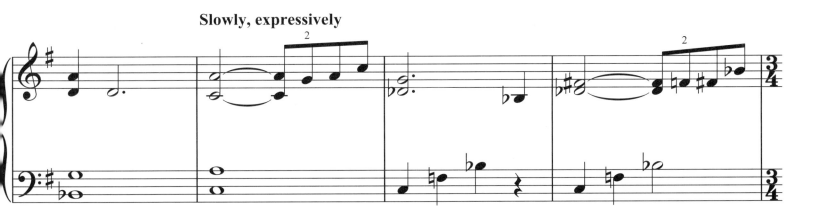

Steadily

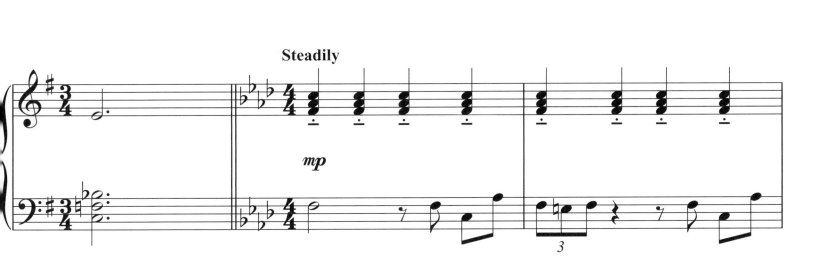

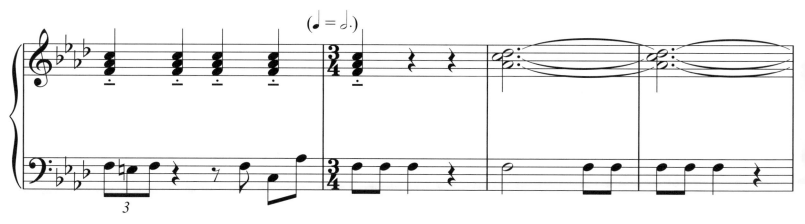

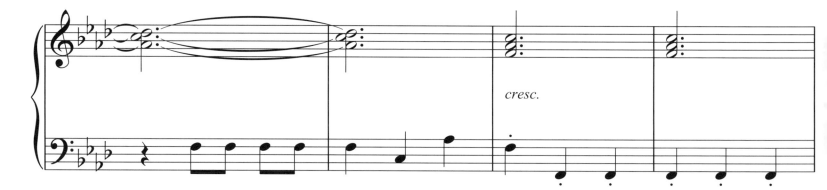

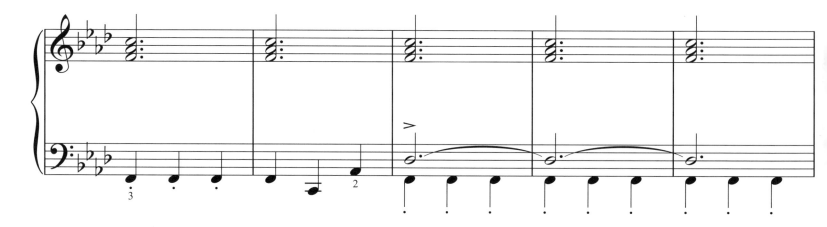

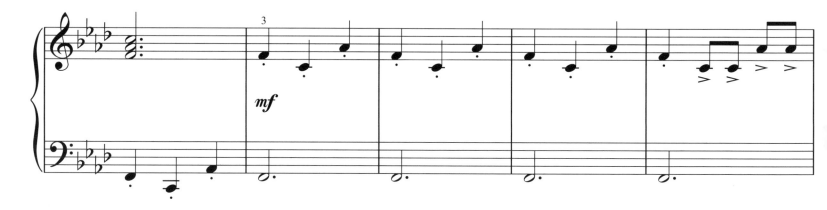

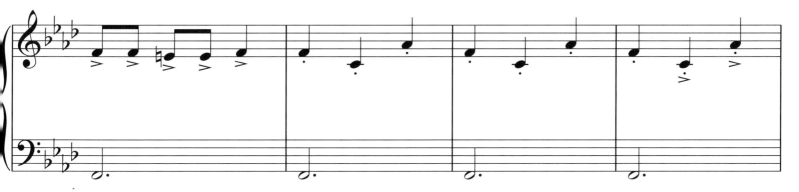

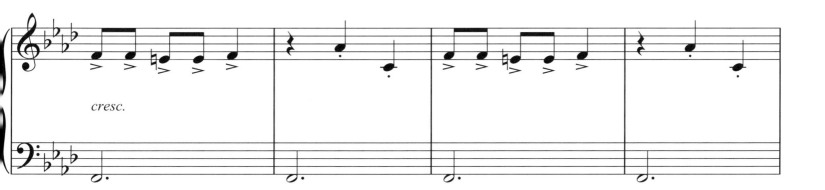

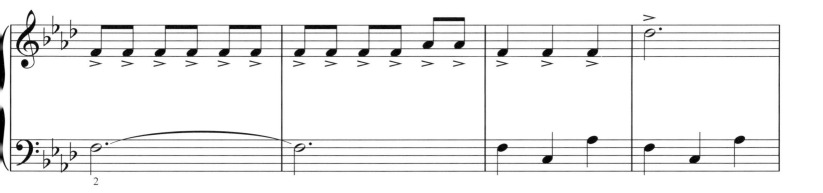

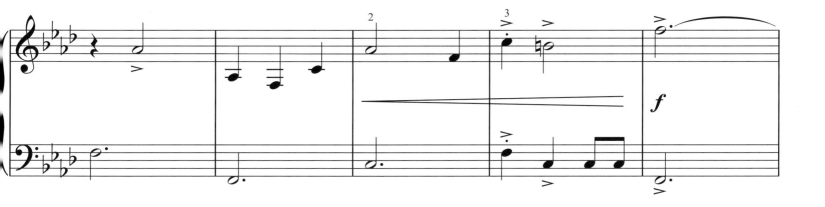

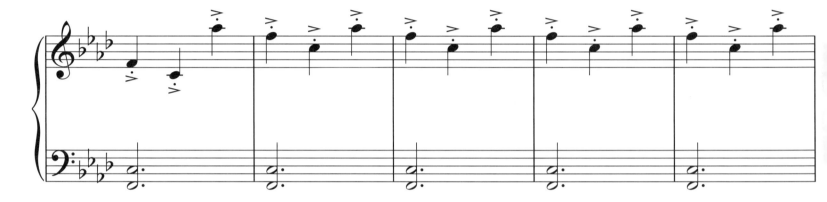

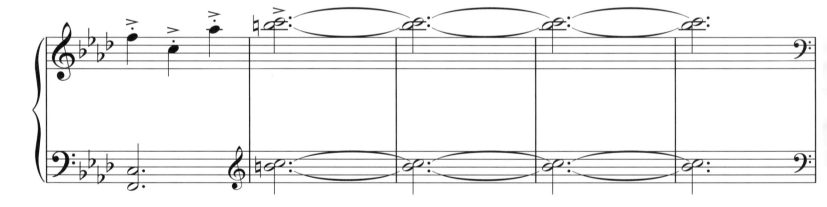

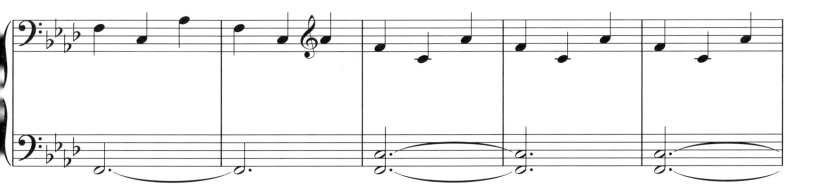

THE LAST JEDI

Music by JOHN WILLIAMS

Moderately, expressively

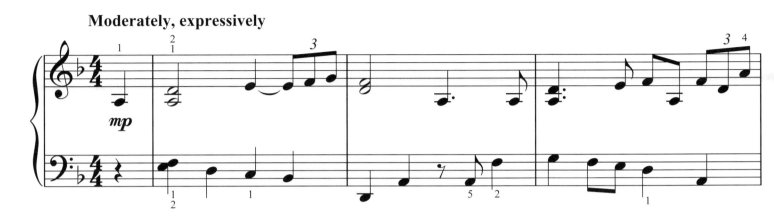

Moderately slow

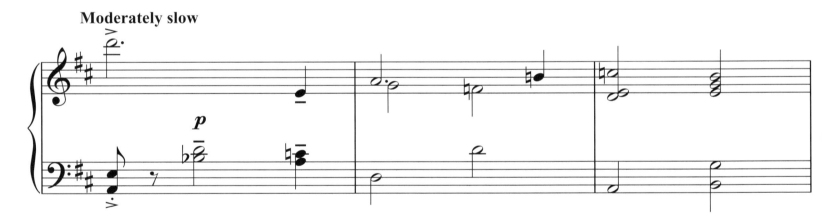

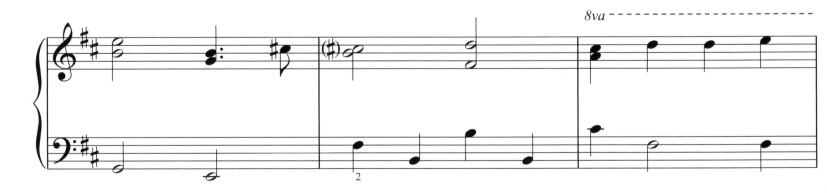

© 2017 Utapau Music, Bantha Music and Warner-Tamerlane Publishing Corp.
All Rights Reserved. Used by Permission.

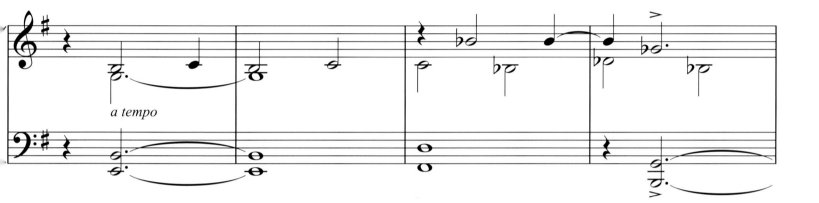

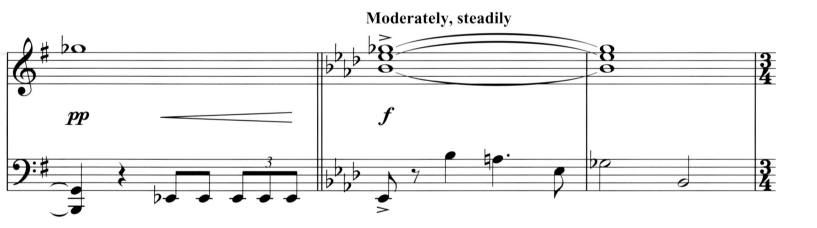

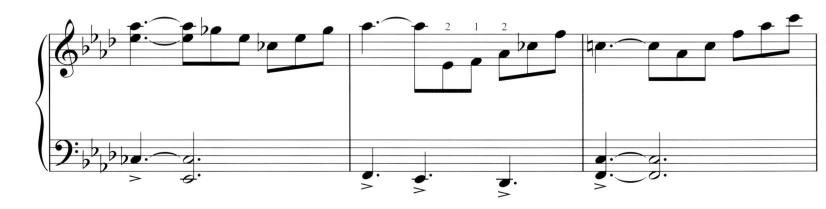

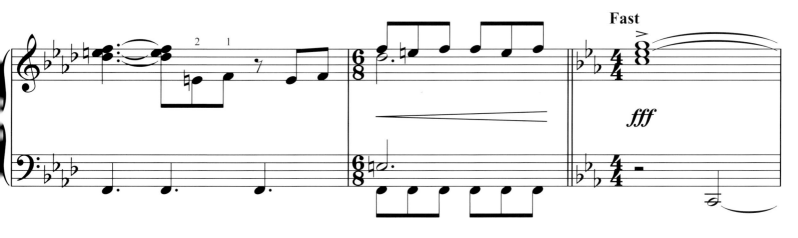

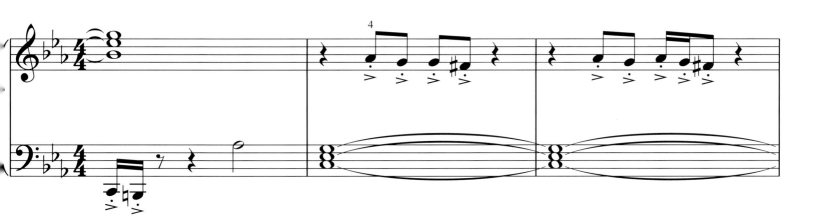

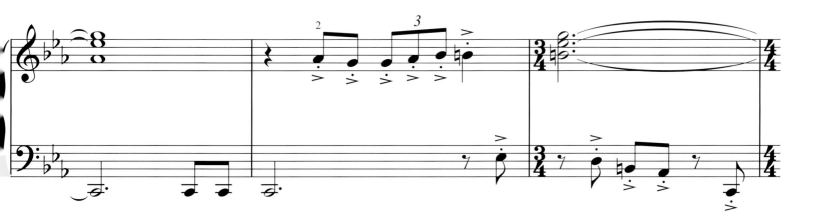

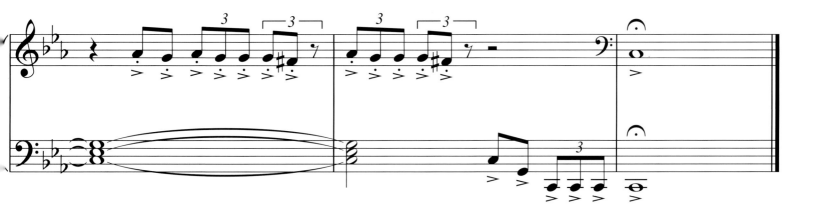

PEACE AND PURPOSE

Music by JOHN WILLIAMS

Moderately slow, expressively

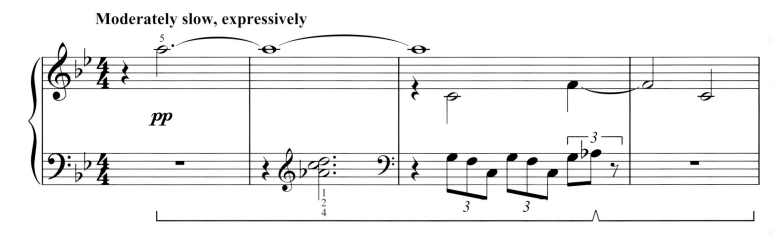

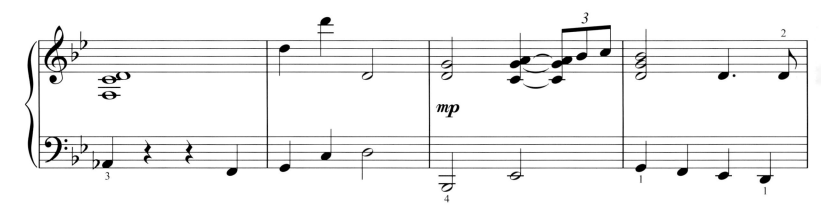

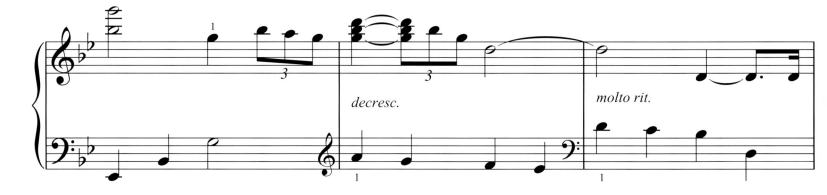

© 2017 Utapau Music, Bantha Music and Warner-Tamerlane Publishing Corp.
All Rights Reserved. Used by Permission.

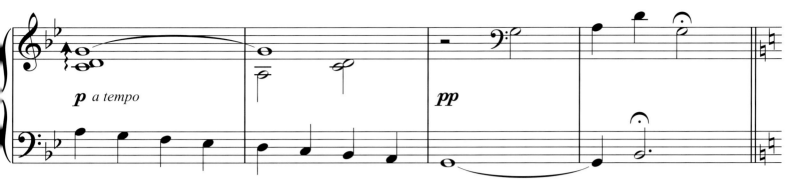

p *a tempo*

pp

Moderately, steadily

f

3

mp

3　*3*　*3*　*3*

62

Moderately fast, steadily